M000290387

POEMS FOR
THE GARBAGE MAN

POEMS FOR THE GARBAGE MAN

by Vinnie Sarrocco

CHATWIN BOOKS
Seattle, 2019

Poems for the Garbage Man, by Vinnie Sarrocco

Text copyright Vinnie Sarrocco (Fiore Vincenzo Sarrocco),
2018–2019. Editorial & design copyright Chatwin Books, 2019.
Edited by Phil Bevis. Book cover by Phil Bevis. Book design by
Annie Brulé.

ISBN (paperback) 978-1-63398-096-9
ISBN (hardcover signed limited) 978-1-63398-097-6

www.chatwinbooks.com

for my mother, Gena

and for everyone
too hungover to make it in
to work today

CONTENTS

POEMS

MUSIC CITY BLUES

Last time I slept
we were strangers.

When the sun rises
oozing tepid rays of humanity
over East Nashville
we will be even stranger.

Our eyes lock for the first time
in the malaise of non-fiction.
No more desperate clinging to
sophomoric abstractions of freedom.
Our manifest mediocrity unmistakable.

You become possessed by
the ghosts of old antebellum street preachers
still grifting around Germantown.
I sit, the naive Protestant
in a Flannery O'Connor story.

Taking the pulpit,
your skinny chest swelling
with Bum Wisdom,

You say:
> sleepin' on the street
> ain't so bad
> you lay down and it's cold
> you wake up
> and it ain't so cold

The Truth of this,
our only anchor
as we drift.

FATALISM IN BLOOM

They gave me an orchid
when my father passed
so that I would have something
of beauty I could watch languidly die—
It is all about perspective

These days she is only a picture
a corolla partly plucked
since the doctors removed her right leg and
left her floating through hospital halls
following phantom footprints in the tile

Fluorescents reflect off a head
radiated into childlike bareness
these were the first pieces of her to go
likely not the last

The petal merchants are all closed
at this hour --
their flora attended only by mist
so I had nothing to offer
aside from my words
and their earnest insincerity

She refuses to give up the ghost
with such confidence
I can almost believe it
someone has to win the lottery or
make up the survival class and be
carried on as statistics in medical journals
why not her

It has been a summer against
a summer littered with the wilted white petals
that Beauty discards so haphazardly
burying us in detritus
seeking to inhale
to draw breath
swell up our chests
and crow into the abyss

BREAKFAST AT SARTRE'S

Start with a glass
of evaporated time
sweeten with brown sugar
thicken into a porridge with tedium

fry futility in pig grease

ignore the pox-like burns on our wrists
and fingers snaked around
one another's throats

smiling—as we do—at the absurdity

smiling and swollen
satisfied enough to
bottle our grins
in monogrammed thermoses

shake them at the sky

shake them at our bosses and landlords
until yesterday emerges
through the spume all fizzled out
wasted carbonation

we who were told
we could be anything
at best can be full

UNTITLED

The cafe
      at 2am
Testing the weight
      just in case

Elbow bending
      sending
A glass on fire
      rocketing towards lips
perfectly pursed in
a Gucci smile

So damn intentional
      the nod
            is for once
convincing

Winking without
      feeling ridiculous

and the walk home
      pregnant
      with
      meaning

More like John Hurt
less like blue balloons
or showers put on
by the boring Aunt
A chest explosion
still echoing
down long Jungian hallways

See it while you can
It'll be too dark
come sun-up

UNION BAR

You writing a song or a love letter?

He asked
            Looking just like the picture of George Clinton
                        hanging over the bar
What's the difference?
I asked
            He smiled
I smiled

Later I heard he was shot
three blocks south
walked back to the bar
and died on that same stool

The messenger so cavalier he
coulda been eulogizing the weather

Welcome to the city
            He said.

Truth is I did feel welcomed

THE SUBSEQUENT YEARS

There are some fogs
so dense, so perennial
that even the proudest of existentialists
will knee concrete
and pray for some divine lantern,
some angelic epiphany,
anything besides this
cellphone's flashlight app
cutting in and out
carving mechanical geometry
out of the haze -
taking the shape of
something like humanity
only less.

These days I mostly use this notebook
to crush fruit flies against the bathroom mirror
until my reflection is so blemished with death
it becomes unrecognizable;
Then prostrate myself on the tile
until I can no longer stand the smell of piss.

Inside it's more like a match
than a lantern,
but I take
what I can get.

FOR THE KIDS

Starting right of peripheral
     like Arabic
only less decipherable
and more arcane:
humming, then wailing.
       A body neglected
lashing out with phantom joint pain.
       Jackson Pollock lungs
predating postmodernism
Meet the new canon,
same as the old canon.
Ernie shows me Loss
in four panels.
Explaining his layering technique -
     irony
           futility
                irony
                     etc.
An obscene lasagna:
something Guy Fieri would slather in BBQ sauce,
drive all the way down
to Flavortown
ignoring the buttery
backseat cries of
"are we there yet?"

There is an inescapable sense of self
cemented and rotting.
Face to face with this decay,
armed with
a century's worth of dada and absurdism,
who would expect
him to be Earnest?

FALLING FOR YOU

The sun tries to set over two bodies
one filled with blood
the other filled with gasoline
only the sun won't ever set
just sits there
in that suspended summer way
southern boys like me
will never get used to

The car idles down Queen Anne's obscene hills;
monarchical monuments
reminding the neighborhood
Mother Nature won't be priced out
pump the brakes
but nothing happens
now at free fall speeds

The possibility of a crash
is neither romantic nor exciting
We're not teenagers anymore
stick and poked
where parents won't see it

There is no smell of fear coming
from the cracked leather passenger seat
which is unsettling
and certainly doesn't bolster my confidence
in the non-existent airbags
removed years ago to make room for naivety
and bricks of cocaine
the border guards didn't bother looking for anyway

I entertain the idea that we could fall like this indefinitely
I entertain the existentialist perspective

and while that wall sure does seems to be getting
closer
who's to say we won't pass right through unscathed
like the white male protagonist
at the end of a Michael Bay film
        mortar and dust just a backdrop
            for a toothy kiss

Don't let physicists lie to you
I hear Bjork whisper in my ear
what other choice do I have but to listen?
separate sets of fingers snake together
the collision is imminent now
        craning my neck
I wait to see if you'll look me in the eyes
and release all the tension in my spine
I heard once that's why drunks tend to survive
their accidents
A different man might imagine heaven
I leave nothing to the imagination
don't call it an ego death
I'd prefer if you didn't call it anything at all.

ANACHRONISM

There was this story about a banana tree
        growing in the West Texas desert
shaking beneath paranormal orbs of light
A silent witness to their magnetic dance
Grand mal movements unburdened by
the subtle paralysis associated with a comfortable
smile
        sung across a counter
                in a place you shouldn't be

I see his truck all around town
but I know it's not
It's a block of cream cheese
on four off road tires
He'd melt before ever hitting Marfa

You say you've had half a bagel today
You say you're body is pulsating
You say it's tattooed in tire tread
There will be no more smiling this afternoon
only arid breeze rustling bananas
and nobody will cry hosanna
even though it's Sunday somewhere

TEXTURED

Hands like corrugated cardboard
coarse and raspy sign language
Goosebumps take shape from your navel
down to your thighs
A less than sterile holiday weekend
extended for months
The lye is pruning your skin
you bitter raisen
       You say:
Grapes grow on vines
and never touch the dirt

The best wine is crushed under bare feet
       You say:
Wine gives me a headache
The taste of contempt lingers on lips
and forms a film around a single long tooth
crystallized into a helpless smile

A follow up wink
hopes to stave off reality
for at least another night

EDEN AS TOBACCO FIELD

A fence of ivory skull fragments
with double socket swing gates
surrounds this garden
where cliches about the lowest fruit
hang next to bushes still burning
from the fires set by anti-Roman barbarians

and sure, the species here are invasive

but the morning glory's pastel countenance
helps to expand irises
on days when it's particularly hard to wake up

and when the tomato vines sprout cans of paste
the metallic shimmer has a sort of charisma
that has to count for something

my mother was so afraid of snakes
that she'd scream during that scene in Indiana Jones
even though she knew it was coming

I've given up trying to understand
why despite such instincts
she tried to reason with the serpent

and instead focus on keeping my blood at the right
temperature
and remembering the subtle differences
        between hugging a loved one
                and constricting prey.

BARROOM SURREALISM

There's an old analog clock
five minutes fast

with interdimensional hands
beyond prehensile

grasping linearly
at narrative structure
as though it were solid and real

hanging over the bar
it's round frame replaces

my face in the mirrored wall

I am a Dali abomination
ticking until I don't

guardian of the liquor

god of the crops
that will ferment into the liquor

I am a just deity
with simple entreaties

please
spare The Virgin

I'll settle for another round
and the T.V. shut off for good

GEOGRAPHY IN MOTION

two sets of teeth
      attached to
            two frames
clenched around an
             ampersand
swinging it ferociously
      like a rabbit
             caught in the jaws
                  of a blue pit
two sets of legs
      pumping in front of
            God and everybody
asses stuck to the yellow rubber seats
      of the swing set
            behind the cabin

do you remember?

MILLENNIAL CONSISTENCY

American diners don't change
no matter how many times
Aunt Harper stands up and sidearms the Heinz
into the wood paneling
glass shattering into infinite
sharpened shards of universe
her eyes glazed with ketchup
or maybe Bloody Mary mix
a noun that can't be swept away
American diners don't change
regardless of area code
or the colors of collars
toast is always toast
even with the addition of avocado
an indulgence the economists say
will snare you in serfdom indefinitely
Aunt Harper doesn't want to talk about the glass
which is good
because nobody asked her to anyway
scribble it on a napkin
file it under A
for American diners
get back to dripping nuclear egg yolk
over your abstract concepts
of what empathy means
in a world governed by potentiality
and mutually assured destruction

IDLING

Sitting on a sunny porch
it's almost like back in Carolina
and all the reasons I had to leave
shrink
like heads in that New Orleans row house
where the Madame expressed
that I would probably prefer not to hear
the results of my tarot reading
I didn't protest
not since Austin Texas
not since Austin Baucom was killed by that
drunk driver on his 23rd birthday
not since I found a new porch to sit
and waste away on while
drowning nostalgia in rotgut whiskey
and practicing
not crying in public

ESSE QUAM VIDERI

new skin cells growing over scar tissue
a body constricted by changing plans
the plain language
to your legal jargon
                    lost in the cacophony
buried beneath glassware
and irony
leave your coif facial hair at home tonight
we're setting off M80s
            in ant mounds
                    by the trailer park
we're catching fireflies in mason jars
            that held moonshine
                    as recently as last night
we're smoking inside
            and we're sorry
                    but we're not embarrassed

ELEGY FOR A DRUG DEALER

He told me how
he visited his grandmother
How she's dying alone
      How desperate she is
for the studio film era American ending
      she immigrated here for

He didn't use so many words

Still I saw a lifetime of banalities
culminating into just another day
I saw a period fall asleep
between two other periods

He told me how
he saw the most vivid reflections in her eyes
and wondered how we can deal
      with the conditional nature
of a concept so abstract
      as consciousness

He didn't use so many words

In fact he used hardly any
but he didn't have to
him being so goddamned consistent
      and all

WHY ECKHART TOLLE IS FULL OF SHIT

No one has transcended the compulsion
If they had
they wouldn't look so lively
They'd sport bovine eyes
        and catatonic lips chiseled into something
                between a smile and scowl
They wouldn't have anything to say to you
        and even if they did
                there'd be no reason to write it down
It's why the first time you learned
        the universe was expanding
                there was a comfortable nausea
The smell of infinity
        superseding the burden of wholeness
                all the way down to your gut

A SPRING TIME POEM

God bless you
God bless you
    alright!
        two's enough
            stop being self-indulgent
spattering fungi
like some kind of theist watchmaker
or new-atheist
Sam Harris neckbeard zealot
and big bang enthusiast

the seasons are changing
and with this great weather
comes great responsibility
so cover your fucking mouth

there's enough bacteria out here
running for office
and reading poetry

FAITH

You and those magpie eyes
perched impossibly high
leering down at
pubescent teenage boys
daring any pockmarked
grubby country scrub
to try it
and see what happens.
I want to remember you
as a crane
long and elegant
brimming with regality.
I want to remember you
as a trailer park pit bull also
loyal to a fault
your working class teeth
tearing away at
the thick Carolina air
or howling at the new moon
but that
would be doing you a disservice.
These are false memories
of a person who only exists in
the smallest of contexts
memories corroded by time
and rewritten.
But I have to
remember you as anything
other than a local news headline.
Faith, I'm not usually keen on
prayer
but I'm praying for your daughter.
I'd pray for justice too,
if I thought there was any left in this world.

THE BEST OF US

You sounded older on the phone
like frogs had been tonguing the honey
hidden in your throat
while I was away.
Earlier that day you performed an ultrasound
on Pete, who ran the old Landmark Tavern
where bikers and hipsters
doctoral candidates and worst of all
lawyers
drank together like some woo woo
Jacque Fresco vision of utopian future
a place that served as a functional home
for me personally.

Pete's waiting on a liver transplant.
You say seeing him
reminded you of me.
The words float in my hand
unburdened by the weight of admonishment
association only in the most benign sense.

Remember when we kissed in the sandbox?
Remember life unadulterated by living?
Just light-up Reeboks
and sand.

Lips still sound like velcro to me
like tearing away
like dial tone
like all the mountains and prairie between us,
all the poison and ambition,
just pieces of dream
that can only form narratives in retrospect.

Looking down on Rainier Avenue,
I know Pete's not gonna make it,
But it's okay.
At least you did.

THE CAR LOT

I remember the grease most of all
dripping from countertops
or fingertips
inside of sinuses
smeared on the faces of mechanics
and the sons of mechanics.
The taste of it on your fingers
like dip spit from a Coke can
tallow hands on my head
a mouth full of wasps
too naive to scream and
let them fly away.

A horizon of used cars
broken glass and gravel
ashtrays overflowing.
Mostly though
I remember the grease.

IN DEFENSE OF THE FERAL

Oughta be something more
than swollen fists clenched
around necks,
and bottlenecks.
Oughta be something more fulfilling
than grinding enamel
and wild eyes peering around
corners
scaring folks in khakis.
Oughta be something tangible.
Something you can sink your teeth
into.
Something that wants to dribble down
your chin
but you don't let it.
Oughta take pride in clean linens,
in sketching out an existence
with a careful tracing hand.
Oughta but isn't.
The Wise Man knows it's all grass
on both sides
the shit dogs eat
when they want to throw up.

ROAD POEM

There's fear flowing
through the ventilation system
poking holes in my psyche
like an ozone layer

Is the alignment shaking the steering wheel
or my hands,
transformed into threatened rattlers
confusing your sedan for a predator

Let's swim in the Mexican snow
Let's abandon our cars on the shoulder
of the untamed desert
and lie in the back seat

connecting the burn marks
carelessly seared into the upholstery
Mapping constellations and finding shapes
more rational than the ones seen on the news

No, best keep west—
stop too soon
and the gas station attendant
will see right through you

THAT'S THE GRAND CANYON ALRIGHT

I used to just think of it as a hole
that the banal dreams
of passionless fathers
haphazardly carved from the earth

But you were right
it is certainly
something

Still
I might have been too hungover
or too busy making sexy eyes at Swedish tourists
to really get the full experience

THOSE WE ARE APT TO FORGET

There was a factory
in Muscle Shoals Alabama
that produced watercolor paintings
made for myopic motel managers

The line workers there
unaware they were even making art
until their brushstrokes
were outsourced to Taiwan

I sat on the floor cross legged
and dreamed of loose teeth
and loose legs
landlines and days off

The lightbulbs in places like this
burn a waxy crayola yellow
and leave a film on the outside of your skin

The pervasive sound
of television static
permeates through all of opiate country.

CAPITAL "T"

I've lost interest
in stalking vague truths
through the paper jungles
stinking up East Texas

I want to look down the sights
of a ballpoint dripping with uncertainty
and take aim at the qualifiers
At West
At Grit
At Car.com
Walmart sells wrapping paper year round
and I have a friend in Raleigh who designs cakes
for dancers to conceal their true intentions

The harshness of humanity
is made more palatable
when it falls gently onto a bed of neuron fibres
the Red Cross traps school supplies in scotch tape
and even nudity
is improved with cake

DATING IN THE MODERN AGE

As if commanded by an impatient universe
The pages stick together
unwittingly bringing their story
one page closer to completion

So I guess it's not that silly
for your image to stay
superimposed on the backs of my eyelids
and the tallest effigy in my dreamscape.

We're tying messages to the backs of wavelengths
like sickly carrier pigeons
frantically trying to figure out
who's patronizing who

Cell phones slip from sweaty hands
crash onto the floor
like fingers on cello strings
playing a ringtone concerto

Let's cut the shit
throw out all previous syntax
and draw pistols instead.

LITTLE FIVE POINTS

Your red balloons cast alien shadows
on the mannequins peering voyeuristically
through the windows of trendy retail shops.
I suppose I looked sympathetic
leaving the anarchist bookstore,
but even with a handful of Chomsky
appealing to my better nature
I still wished you would have walked
in a different direction.
Maybe if we hadn't made eye contact
I could have slipped inside the cinder blocks
and pretended to buy a $25 T-shirt
with a Banksy print stenciled on the front.
Instead, we'll have coffee
and you'll say all the things
I'd prefer you not to,
and I'll promise to take you
as far as Nashville
but we both know the best I can do
is purchase your overpriced percocet
and stand in solidarity
behind the Punk Rock Pizza place,
crushing corporate hegemony
into thin white lines
I'll snort off books with ideas
that I'm too weak to put into practice.

RAINIER AT SUNUP

it was at the Hearse Depot
across from your therapist
where I learned to see
the birds again
the two blues
in cliche sorrowful love
the bowed-up crows
vomit braggadocio in the street
braving traffic for succulent trash
migrating
from mortuary to mortuary
the sky
the only thing
separating us from them

POSTCARD POEM 1

death is reasonable
     consistent
usually quiet
while guardian angels
 tend to make poor house guests
          and never show up on time

POSTCARD POEM II

I will keep reading the books
the girls with defiant eyes
blue hair and reluctant smiles
                    recommend
until I figure out
if they've learned to float
or if their soles
are just too heavy
to touch the earth

POSTCARD POEM III

They call it the sweet science
but boxing is more like
      poetry
There is discovery
      only self discovery
The kind you can't find
in graduated cylinders

POSTCARD POEM IV

Most people think of love
in a 4/4 time signature
sung by British pop stars
or bowed out on strings

In actuality it's polyrhythmic
avant-garde noise funk
guys with mustaches
pretend to like

POSTCARD POEM V

We take isopropyl breaths
      and pretend to spit fire
We watch the the boy
      the innocence stolen from his eyes
drop to his knees
      in the middle of a tobacco field
quoting Conrad

This is the beginning
of an East coast
West coast
rap beef
between himself
and God

GROCERY LIST

I

I must remember to get the orange juice.
More importantly,
I must remember to see the beauty
in the simple
going and fetchings.
Like O'Hara's oranges—
His Coke
shared with lips like those
you wear to bed.
The plums in the icebox.
It doesn't have to be
so serious
so palliative.

II

My mother took pride
in smelling the rain in the wind
before even the clouds.
Before even her God.
Today I got a whiff of nostalgia.
It smelled like the sound
grass makes as it surrenders
under mower blades
and is trampled beneath tractor tires.
It smelled like thunder—
like country colloquialisms about bowling.
When the morning dew collects
itself on the concrete
I will remember the shape of your haircut,
and that I've forgotten the orange juice.

III

If there were crepe myrtles
outside my window
I imagine I could write a lovely poem
called *crepe myrtles*
and I wouldn't have to write the word death
in it, even once.
As it stands, there are only condos,
garbage dumpsters and human feces.
The air is filled with the city's frustrations.
It is thick with too many molecules.
The carrion choke on it,
gulls gasp and scream
at the sun as it rises
scintillating over the sound.
They are my tearful, flying crepe myrtles.
crying out and shitting on the cement.
dropping their panicles at the end of summer.

IV

There is one sea bird in particular
teeming with virility
though his feathers are grey.
He stands in the middle of First Avenue
four feet tall
duck-footed, daring any car
or lawyer to get froggy.
Truly, I believe he would stand unflinching
and statuesque, a testament
to Man's ineffectuality
while some hipster's Jetta
would be left with a comically
gull-shaped dent in the front bumper.
A clash of egos worthy of a renaissance fresco.

V

The sun has given up the go-getter
summer mania in favor of
mild autumnal depression.
Today I rise before it,
mocking the dark
with each steel-toed thud
of boots on linoleum.
The grey gull watches
from his weathervane perch
as I pour water into a juice glass
in defeat. The day is casting its ensemble.
The rest of the crying trees sleep.
It's too early to shed their blossoms.

ELEGY FOR A COMEDIAN

You entered a place that light could not
that words about light could not
you cowered beneath artificial coruscation
or worse yet fluorescent murmurs
echoing off concrete ceilings
the reverberations trapped between
your blood-dried nostrils
and the part of your head
where the hair began to thin
stood naked and hunched
an autopsy report pacing erratically
back and forth
wild-eyed spilling its contents
into a spit-riddled karaoke mic
petulant and screaming:

it's okay
I'm not okay
but it's funny
or at least
I hope you will
tell me it is

and they would sometimes
and it was enough sometimes
and the scintillating small-town moon
would float you to bed
and you could sleep sometimes
wake and face another day
in that place that light could not enter
that words about light could not enter

WITNESS TO A BURNING

Where there is smoke
There is fire

She wakes
lumbers over pallets
and repurposed scrap

to become one with the ash
a symphony of particles
and synonyms for solipsism

No stranger to the blaze

the conflagration in her soul
manifests externally
consuming the hills in all directions

pinnacled now on a single vertex
not in the flames crawling up her sides

in her scream
a shrieking howl so primal
so largely ignored

I am reminded of what a burden
cognizance can be
and how ephemeral
the smoke can seem

THERE'S NOTHING FUN TO DO
IN HOUSTON

I had never seen a Picasso
in person before
as I stood in admiration
the room was swarmed
by a pride of middle school children
their wild dilated eyes bulging from their sticky heads
intoxicated on the weekday air

an exasperated teacher
sashayed behind
asking rhetorical questions
about geometry
and it's relation to anatomy
her words assertive
bored and rehearsed
fogged the air
      see the triangles?
      the squares?
      the circles?
I leaned towards a boy
      muttered
            the circles are tits

the teacher wasn't amused
but I bet Pablo would have enjoyed the levity

EULOGY

He was a man
whose keys were
persistently slipping
off their metallic band
a magnet for ghosts
that once belonged
to benign pranksters/
The kind of guy
who finds himself
in sentences
he's yet to read
but will someday/
A man with too many
bones rattling around
beneath thin skin
clanking down hallways
audible only in the
sounds of humming fans
and ambient low whispers
of those with nothing
interesting to say
He was/
Mostly.

NEOTERIC SKYLINES

a new city the same wood
the same rats gnawing
on new electrical cords
crawling up the same pant legs
of new bar patrons
new to you at least

past iterations of self
bloom and fall away
like cigarette ash into
a novelty Joe Camel ashtray
some things have a way of landing
perfectly in place
like the ouroboros tail
not often
but sometimes

this is the cheese
        you reckon
at the end of the maze
        you reckon for now
you'll reckon with the stillness
        the languor
homes are built on

HOW TO CONVINCE KIDS IN PUNK-HOUSES YOU'RE COOL

wake up with splinters
in your puffy cheeks
from the kitchen subflooring
also known colloquially as
    The Bedroom
your legs are less than sturdy
gut full of yesterday's Mickeys
head of hot coals
and nothing left to burn but the bedsheets

you've given up on normalcy
normalcy is dog speak
for bourgeois decadence
you tell yourself;
you tell your aunt
at your nephew's christening

you buy a gun
burn your fingerprints off
       on an electric stove
sell cocaine to the kids
at the local state college

you smoke in airports
and fight often
you drool disdain for ties and khakis
then die
young
never once feeling free from anything
despite all your hollerin'
so you ask for an epitaph

made of dry erase instead of stone
'cause freedom only seems to exist in other people's
words
and you have no permanent home

FUNERAL FOR A MAN

there is the morning

steeped in the aftermath of emergency
you cram between two round midwestern bodies

sweating travel through their suits
and Hawaiian shirts respectively they are
someone else's fathers

they do not yield the brass foot rail

there is a Dewars and water
flesh blackened by time
drips from the bartender's eyes
into the ice
you smell of yesterday's medicine

keep your arms at your sides careful not to hear
the sounds a family makes
through someone else's cell phone

There is the boarding
pressurized cabin
air floods your sinuses
you are asphyxiating

on other people's breath
the repose offered by your dirt

replaced by
someone else's sky
there is a soaring

ethereal weightlessness   you are
an extra in someone else's fugue

state   two children speak only in screams
bounce feet against the back of your seat
endless misapplied protest to confinement
they can't understand

There is the debarkation   blood returns
to your legs in commemoration of this
homecoming

you are raw and pink   swimming
upstream towards the jet bridge
struggling against other people's
luggage

you leave one panopticon
and enter another   sterile white bricks
remind you of a time before
remembering

you are baptized in an olfactory cascade:
Jello, industrial cleaner, decaying bodies
in palliative care kept alive for someone else's benefit

There is a man in scrubs whose emanations
of comfort are as sincere
as they can be for someone who is paid
to be comforting   he brings you into a room
says your father can hear you
though he can't speak, or move, or breathe
and occupies someone else's skin

There are someone else's hands
You remember
bricks
in reverse
but they have shrunken now

or maybe you've been inflated
they are warm
and that is something

you will apologize since he is incapable
it will float face down
in the sticky hospital air the nurse will turn off
the machines

there will be gluttonous consumption   you will leave
behind a mausoleum made of ham bones and liquor bottles
and other people's casserole dishes
it is an act

of cyclical defiance against an all consuming natural order
that demands a mirror be held against it

there is a box of ashes

much heavier than you imagined when it comes time
to scatter them it will take much longer
than T.V. has lead you to believe
He will be spilled in concentric circles   around
other people's dolor   his residue
will stain your hands and some else's
dress-shirt   it is almost
intimate

There is the mourning.

ACKNOWLEDGEMENTS

Special thanks to Maged Zaher, Robert P. Kaye, Steve Sibra, Erika Brumett, and everyone in the Seattle poetry scene that has supported me for the last two years.

Thanks to my sister Nicole who is a constant inspiration to me.

Thanks to Rebecca Huvard for her love and support, and for putting up with my early mornings and late nights.

Thanks to Phil Bevis, Annie Brulé, Cyra Jane Hobson, and the team at Chatwin Books for creating such beautiful books, and making this one happen.

Thanks to the editors of the following publications where the following poems first appeared:

Rue Scribe: "Eulogy"
Behold Magazine: "How to Convince Kids in Punk-houses
    You're Cool"
SPREAD: "Neoteric Skylines"
Coffin Bell: "Fatalism in Bloom"

CPSIA information can be obtained
at www.ICGtesting.com
Printed in the USA
FFHW022208300519
52732448-58268FF

9 781633 980969